2WM Q

300·72

**The Student's Guide to**

*Preparing*
*Dissertation*
*and Theses*

**The Student's Guide Series from Kogan Page**

# The Student's Guide to

# *Preparing Dissertations and Theses*

## BRIAN ALLISON

KOGAN
PAGE

First published in 1997
Reprinted 1998, 1999

Kogan Page Limited
120 Pentonville Road
London N1 9JN

**British Library Cataloguing in Publication Data**

A CIP record for this book is available from the British Library.

ISBN 0 7494 2193 2

Typeset by Kogan Page
Printed and bound in Great Britain by Clays Ltd, St Ives plc

# Contents

**List of Figures**

# Preface

This book is written for students following courses in which a dissertation or thesis is an important part of the course or examination requirements. It is applicable to most subject fields in different institutions and countries. Apart from being designed to help students in what is invariably a hurried and tense part of their studies, it is also intended to relieve course tutors and research supervisors from having to respond to endless questions about what are often little more than very routine matters.

Although of different origins, the terms 'dissertation' and 'thesis' have come to be used synonomously and they are used as such in this guide. The material here is based on an earlier publication which was revised a number of times to ensure that it answered the kinds of questions students raise about the formalities of dissertation or thesis preparation. Students' comments and queries, therefore, contributed a great deal to the form and content. Advice and comments from colleagues have also been most helpful in developing this book. It conforms to the recommendations of the British Standards Institute BS4821.

During the last 20 years there have been significant changes in the awarding of research and other higher degrees in the United Kingdom that have affected dissertation or thesis preparation. In addition to those offered by the universities, the Council for National Academic Awards was responsible for a number of advanced and higher degree courses in polytechnics and other institutions of higher education. The Council issued regulations for theses or dissertations presented for the award of research degrees. With the demise of the C.N.A.A. in 1992, the polytechnics and some other institutions of higher education formerly validated by the Council were granted university status and were required by circumstance to develop their own research degree regulations, although, in many cases, they substantially continued the practices developed by the C.N.A.A. The requirements for the presentation of dissertations and theses are often specified in these regulations but they tend to focus on such matters as the expected numbers of words and the procedures for submission, rather than the form of the dissertations or theses. The procedures laid out here are likely to fulfil the expectations for dissertation presentation in most institutions.

Other developments have taken place in recent years which affect the production of dissertations and theses as well as other forms of research reports. These include the increased access to computer technology, particularly word-processors, database programmes and desktop publishing facilities, as well as the increased availability of photocopying and other means of graphic reproduction. Similarly, the increased accessibility of reference material in non-book media, notably through computer technology such as e-mail and the Internet, has had to be accommodated within the system of bibliographical referencing. While the major forms for referencing such material are described in this guide, it is worth noting that more exhaustive coverage is given in the revised edition of *Electronic Style: a guide to citing electronic information*, by Li and Crane (1996, Westport, CT: Mecklermedia).

With advancements in multimedia technology, there is the possibility of students in some institutions being able to submit dissertations or research reports in other than paper formats, such as on CD-ROM or other disk-based materials. While it is beyond the brief of this book to lay out how the technological aspects of such material should be managed and presented, it can be taken that the structure of the research report and the presentation of the text-based material included in the presentation should follow the procedures described here.

A further development has been the formulation of examination regulations that permit the main body of material submitted for assessment to be in some form of practical work, such as may be presented in an exhibition. In such cases, the procedures laid down in this guide should be followed not only for the submission of any substantive documentation required to accompany the work but also for any literal documentation, such as labelling or textual explanations, supporting the practical work submitted. It is normally required that submissions of this kind include a permanent record of the work, such as in the form of photographs or video tapes, submitted with, or as part of, the dissertation. In this case, the procedures laid down here for the inclusion of appendices (pp.32–34) should be followed.

This book is intended to be used as a working document and, as far as possible, the layout of the text itself has been presented as an example for dissertation presentation. This guide, therefore, may also be of use to course tutors as well as research supervisors and examiners, by providing a model against which dissertation presentation may be assessed.

Brian Allison, 1996

# Introduction

A dissertation or thesis is a research report. This guide is designed to help students, and others who are inexperienced in preparing a dissertation or thesis, to overcome some of the main problems of format and style that frequently occur. A dissertation or thesis is, however, only a medium through which research is reported and, of course, the research itself is the most important matter. No matter how well a research report is presented, the value of the report will be dependent upon the quality of the research that is being reported.

A great deal of support is already available to help both the novice and experienced researcher to acquire knowledge and experience in the ways research can be carried out. Most of the research carried out in the natural and social sciences assumes a 'positivistic' stance, based on the postulates of natural kinds, constancy and determinism. Positivistic research subscribes to the 'scientific method', which proceeds from the identification of a problem to the analysis of the problem, the formulation of hypotheses and the testing of those hypotheses, initially by deduction and subsequently by action. An alternative approach, developed particularly, but not exclusively, within the social sciences, is the 'phenomenological' or 'naturalistic' approach, which assumes any situation to be unique. Naturalistic research does not subscribe to the 'scientific method' and is characterised most often by description that cannot be generalised.

The variety of methods through which research can be pursued generally fall into a number of main categories:

- comparative research;
- descriptive research;
- experimental research;

- historical research;
- naturalistic research;
- philosophical research;
- practical research.

The particular procedures and strategies implicit in all of these methods have been developed through practice over long periods of time. Clearly, the kind of research question being asked determines the principal method through which it can be answered and, reciprocally, a particular research method being used prescribes the kind of question for which an answer may be sought. In practice, although a particular research project may be pursued through one of the principal research methods, it is likely that aspects of the project will require more than one method to be employed. For example, most social science surveys using descriptive research methods require an historical enquiry into the circumstances leading to the situation being surveyed and a philosophical analysis of the issues being investigated.

The established procedures for these various methods provide indispensable frameworks to guide students in the ways of formulating research questions, developing relevant research designs, selecting appropriate enquiry methods, choosing or devising research instruments and tools and deciding upon ways of analysing data.

## The Contexts of Research

In addition to the acquisition of research skills and the practice of various research methods, there are two matters of considerable importance to the student: the selection of a research topic and, relatedly, knowing about the various forms in which research is reported.

## Sources of research topics

Any research project begins with a topic, which may be either in the form of a question being asked or a problem that needs to be solved. As the research topic is of primary importance, one of the biggest dilemmas for would-be researchers is what to research into or, in other words, where to find a research topic. Finding a worthwhile topic is not easy, particularly as identifying a previously unexamined question invariably requires a comprehensive understanding of the subject field, which few students are likely to have. However, finding a topic need not be overly stressful if the task is undertaken systematically and with common sense. In general, there are five main sources for research topics and these apply to all disciplines:

- the 'felt need';
- the literature of the subject field;
- research supervisors;
- institutional research;
- commissioned research.

It is very important to note that any of the five sources described may be used to identify a topic for research. They are all valid sources and one is not more important than, or preferable to, any of the others.

### The 'felt need'

A topic from this source originates with the researcher who identifies a problem as a consequence of experience in, and some considerable knowledge of, the field. This quite often comes from an observed discrepancy or a nagging feeling that something is 'wrong' or problematic. This feeling might arise, for example, because of some unusual or otherwise unaccountable behaviour in a technical or chemical process, or from an observation of the way some people behave for which there is no ready explanation. Examples of the former might be Isaac Newton's enquiries into gravity, which followed his wonderment at why the apple falling on his head hit him with a particular amount of force, or Archimedes' research into the measurement of the volume of irregular solids, following his observation of the rise in the water level as he climbed into the bath. Examples of the latter might come from a teacher's observation that many more boys than girls opt for technology or computer science courses, or an art gallery curator's observation that the number of people in the gallery varies with the time of day.

**The literature of the subject field**
The literature of the subject field is an important source of research topics. The text books and research journals for any subject describe what is already known about the subject and, therefore, can also indicate the gaps in knowledge. Quite often there are conflicting theories or there may be disagreement about how particular phenomena can be explained. An example of conflicting theories from the field of psychology relates to why children draw the way they do: there is the theory that 'Children draw what they know' which appears to be diametrically opposed to the other theory that 'Children draw what they see'. This apparent conflict would be worthy of research.

Research reports, whether they are reports submitted for academic qualifications as dissertations or theses, or reports published by professional research organisations, are a vital part of the literature of any field. Summary research reports or abstracts are regularly published in research journals such as *Nature, Chemical Abstracts* or *Studies in Art Education*. Research reports in the form of dissertations or theses submitted by students for MPhil and PhD research degrees are normally held by the library of the university or college. Almost every research report includes a section with a heading something like 'Possibilities for future research'. This section of a research report often refers to questions that arose during the research project but were unanswered either because they were outside the scope of the project or because there was insufficient time to pursue them. Building upon previous research and following up questions raised in earlier researches is one of the most important sources of professional research activity.

A good grasp of the kinds of research topics pursued in a subject can be gained by carrying out searches of specialist subject research indexes. Research indexes, which may be in book form or accessible on computer, are normally held in the library, as described later in this guide. It is worth looking at the titles of completed research reports listed in the indexes to see how they have been formulated. Some titles are very precisely formulated whereas others are vague. With familiarity with the subject, it might be possible to identify from the indexes those areas or topics that have been well-researched, and those that have been minimally researched. It may even be possible to infer topics that have yet to be studied.

### Research supervisors

All student research is guided by members of staff acting as research supervisors. Some departments in universities and higher education colleges have appointed readers or professors, and these posts indicate a departmental responsibility for research, which usually includes the appointment of supervisors for student research projects. Supervisors are generally experienced both as research supervisors and as active researchers. As it is necessary to have a supervisor, it is equally necessary to identify a research topic that falls within the interest of, or is at least within the competence of, staff in the department who are responsible for research supervision. There have been many examples of potential research students who have proposed very worthwhile topics but have not been able to pursue them because they have not been able to find suitable supervisors. It makes sense, therefore, to find out what topics are of interest to possible supervisors before finalising a research topic. It is often the case that potential supervisors can draw upon their knowledge of current research and help research students identify worthwhile topics for research.

### Institutional research

Research that is already going on in a subject department or school is a major source of new research topics. Many departments or schools support research being carried out both by tutors and students, including those working for research

5

degrees. Identifying a research topic that links in with what others in the same department are doing is very helpful in all kinds of ways. Research is an essentially collaborative endeavour and it is extremely encouraging and supportive to be able to talk about a research project and share ideas with others working in the same field. Some departments with a developed research ethos have active 'programmes of research', in which a number of researchers and research students work on different aspects of the same research problem. Checking out what is already being done in a department can lead to the identification of new but related topics. If the proposed research work is highly specialised, most of the equipment necessary to pursue a related topic will already be available.

**Commissioned research**
Experienced researchers often undertake projects into topics that have been identified by others. Research that has been commissioned by industry or local and national organisations and bodies constitutes a substantial proportion of all research activity. Good examples of such research are the surveys or opinion polls carried out by research companies into all kinds of political and other attitudes and opinions. Similarly, most commercial companies, such as those selling washing powders or motor cars, undertake some kind of market research before launching a new product. On a wider scale, the National Foundation for Educational Research is a body that is commissioned by the government and a variety of other agencies to enquire into many aspects of educational provision and practice. In these cases, the general topic is identified by the commissioning body or organisation, and the researchers develop this into a workable research project. This includes developing the research instruments, such as questionnaires, interview schedules or tests, and deciding to whom to address the enquiries. A different kind of example is research into a particular technical process or development, which may be commissioned by, say, a chemical or engineering company. In all these examples, the researchers are employing

their research experiences and skills to investigate issues in which they do not have a vested interest. Many departments in institutions of higher education undertake commissioned research and, quite frequently, this forms the basis for research degree work and is used as a research training for students, sometimes as part of partnership schemes between education and industry.

## Reporting Research Outcomes

The reporting of research outcomes is an essential part of the research endeavour and it can be argued that it is one of the crucial characteristics which distinguish research from non-research. It can also be argued that research cannot be said to have been carried out, or was not worth carrying out, unless someone else, other than the researcher, can learn from it. The main purpose of the research report, such as a dissertation or thesis, is to communicate not only the outcomes of the research but also, of equal importance, information about the purposes, methods and techniques underpinning the research. The research report makes the research accessible to others and, by doing so, places the research in the public domain. The accumulated body of research reports in a subject field constitutes, to a large degree, the body of knowledge which is the subject field.

Recognising the need to build upon the existing knowledge in a subject field and then contributing to that body of knowledge characterise what may be termed a *professional attitude to research*. The first aspect of a professional attitude to research is the acceptance that the project needs to be developed in the *overt recognition* of previous research, and builds on it. Being familiar with previous research, not only in terms of the particular and related topics but also in terms of the wide range of methods and strategies that may be of relevance, is a necessary pre-condition to any form of research. Indeed, it is not only poor research but also a waste of valuable time

7

to pursue questions that have already been answered or to devise strategies or instruments when tried and tested ones are already available. There are no medals for re-inventing the wheel.

The second aspect of the professional research attitude is acceptance of the responsibility to report the outcomes of any research to the subject field. (As may be appreciated, the first aspect is dependent on the second.) There are a number of reasons why this is important, not least that it renders the project open to critical appraisal by others in the field. Such appraisal is not only essential to the further development of the researcher's own understanding but it also makes an important contribution to that of others, including the appraisers. Nevertheless, reporting research to the field can have complications. Some researchers in education and industry, for example, whose work has direct commercial or financial implications, feel that such reporting might leave their work open to exploitation by competitors. However, providing that patenting and other intellectual property rights safeguards are utilised, this should not be a major problem. Far more important is the value of participating in a shared professional endeavour.

Research reports take a number of different forms and these are determined, to a large extent, by the intended audience or readership. Research reports to be presented at conferences and printed in conference proceedings may be structured in a different way to those which are to be read in academic or professional journals. Similarly, research reports submitted for academic awards in the form of theses or dissertations may differ from those submitted to a client at the end of a commissioned research project. The format of research reports, therefore, may differ in terms of such matters as length, detail, style of writing, order of content, tables, figures, appendices and so on.

Research reports are meant to be read and, therefore, knowing about the main forms in which research is reported helps to make such reading more efficient. Research reports written by students, apart from showing their interest in and understanding of the topic of their researches, are intended to demonstrate that they have mastered some or all aspects of research methodology. This demonstration of mastery is the main basis on which they are assessed by tutors, supervisors or examiners. Reports produced by experienced researchers, of course, can be expected to be underpinned by a mastery of research methods. The critical reading and appraisal of such research reports by other professionals in the particular field of research is a normal part of the research endeavour.

The four forms of research report that are readily accessible to students, are:

- student research reports;
- research reports in journals;
- research abstracts;
- research indexes.

## Student research reports

Students write research reports for a variety of purposes and at various times during their studies at school, college or university. For many students, the culmination of their student research activity and their entry into the career level of professional research is the submission of a research report as a dissertation or thesis in partial or total fulfilment of the requirements for a MPhil or PhD research degree. Some dissertations resulting from the individual research requirements of taught Master's degree courses are at a similarly high level. Although the depth of content of a research project may vary from, for example, that carried out in school or at undergraduate level to that expected of a doctorate, the standard of presentation of a dissertation or thesis needs to be consistently high.

## Research journals

The publication of research reports in professional journals is characteristic of most subject fields that engage in advanced work. Most of these journals are published under the aegis of professional bodies or subject associations and, as many of these have a national and international readership, the quality of the contents is usually very high. Many editorial boards use expert 'referees' to review articles or reports submitted for consideration for publication and judge whether or not they are of a sufficiently high standard to be published.

In most cases, professional journals have an adopted 'house style', which covers specifications for presentation in terms of layout, length, form of illustration, use of footnotes, bibliographical referencing system and so on. These specifications and other information about the submission of articles for publication are usually given in the journals.

## Research abstracts

Abstracts or summaries of research reports are an important part of the research literature. They are important because they provide brief overviews of what is often extensive and detailed documentation and enable researchers and others to decide which reports are of direct interest to them and are therefore worthy of further reading.

Writing an abstract is a difficult task as it requires the condensation of possibly tens of thousands of words into a few hundred. Depending on the nature of the research, abstracts can usually be expected to outline: the purposes of the research and its contexts; the hypotheses, if any, being tested; the subjects or samples taking part in the research; the research methods adopted; the major conclusions; and the relevance to the field.

Writing abstracts of completed research is an essential part of research practice. Students completing research degrees are required to provide abstracts of their researches, which are included in the dissertations and theses. Similarly, many journals require abstracts to be provided as introductory sections to articles submitted for publication.

## Research indexes and databases

Research indexes or databases are categorised listings and summaries of researches in specialist fields and, as such, represent the most direct routes to research information. *Chemical Abstracts*, for example, is reputed to be the largest book in the world with over half a million new entries annually. The entries in many indexes, such as the *Aslib Index to Theses* and the *Allison Research Index of Art and Design*, include abstracts that have been written specifically for them.

Research indexes are usually printed as hard copy in book form, but increasingly they are being made available in a computerised form. The computerisation of indexes has not only made information about research more readily accessible, nationally and internationally, but has also made searching the databases available in this form a relatively easy matter. Computerised databases are available either on disk (floppy or CD-ROM) or 'on-line'. The databases on disk are accessible using computers or computer terminals held in the library or department. The periodic updating of these databases is achieved by the publication of new editions of the disks. On-line databases, which may be national or international, may be located anywhere in the world, and are accessed using a telecommunication system through a computer or computer terminal usually held in the library or department. Some of these databases are accessible through the Internet, using a modem, which links a computer to a telephone line, or by a direct telephone line. It is usual for on-line databases to be updated frequently, often on a daily basis, as new information is fed into them. Guidance from a librarian or tutor is usually needed to access on-line databases.

Information about researches given in indexes is usually classified into a number of 'fields'. Not all databases use the same format but, in general, one can expect to find the following fields:

- name(s) of researcher(s);
- title of project;
- year of completion;
- academic qualification, if any, for which the research was submitted, and the awarding body;
- the duration of the project;

- the institution in which the research was carried out and the sponsors, if any;
- details of publications, if any, arising from the research;
- a brief description of the project in the form of an abstract;
- key words describing the project to enable identification and retrieval.

## Searching indexes and databases

A key feature of databases is that they can be 'searched' to provide specific information and, of course, this is much easier and faster with computerised databases than with those published in book form. Most of those published in book form provide cross-referenced keyword and subject lists to assist searches. With computerised databases, depending on the particular database programme that has been used, searches can be carried out by entering the search requirements in one or more fields and the searches are then carried out automatically. Key words are extremely useful for carrying out general searches on topics of interest and databases can usually be searched by stipulating a number of relevant key words. For example, undertaking a search using the key words INDUSTRIAL DESIGN, EXPERIMENTAL would find all projects in Industrial Design that employed an experimental research method. This broad search could be narrowed down by specifying further key words such as INDUSTRIAL DESIGN, EXPERIMENTAL, FURNITURE, DISABLED, ERGONOMICS in order to find experimental industrial design studies which focus on the ergonomics of furniture designed specifically for disabled people.

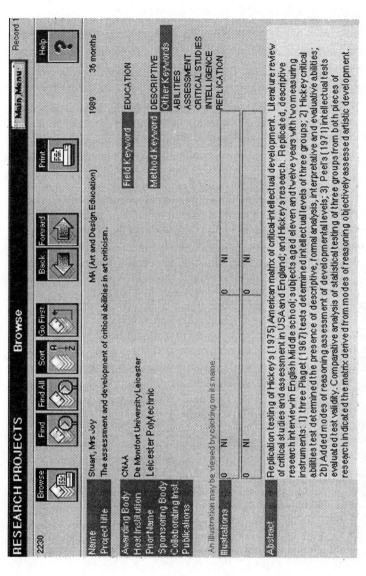

**Figure 1:** *Example of a database entry (Allison, 1996)*

13

## Preparing a Dissertation or Thesis

There are a variety of ways in which the products of a study or investigation can be prepared for presentation as a dissertation or thesis. The form in which the material is presented is the vehicle for the communication of ideas and information and, as such, should be recognised as a means rather than an end. Until relatively recently, it was assumed that dissertations and theses would be typewritten, but it is now accepted that they may be either typewritten or word-processed and this book describes appropriate alternative forms of presentation. Some word-processors allow for the choice of typefaces and font sizes similar to that formerly exclusive to the typesetter. This facility enables *italics*, for example, to be included in the text whereas, when typewritten, the italicising of words, such as in bibliographic referencing, is indicated by <u>underlining</u>. Similarly, the fonts in some word-processor programmes include mathematical and other symbols which otherwise require the use of specialised typewriters. The use of a word-processing facility, however, should conform to normal typesetting standards and be directed solely at the clarification of the text. It should not be used for mere whimsy or decoration.

It is helpful to be clear about the purposes of academic theses and dissertations as well as to bear in mind the intended readership. It is somewhat salutary to realise that most theses and dissertations have an intended readership of only two or, sometimes, three readers – that is, the external and internal examiners – although, of course, they may be read subsequently by many others.

Generally speaking, the purpose of the assessment of any research report submitted for an academic award, whether it is at undergraduate or postgraduate level, is that it is the assessment of the student's abilities to:

- identify a problem;
- analyse the problem;
- carry out appropriate literature and other searches in a methodical way;

- develop a research design employing relevant research methods or strategies;
- select or devise appropriate data-collecting instruments that are valid and reliable;
- implement the design in practice using, if appropriate, samples selected on relevant criteria;
- collate and analyse data using appropriate techniques;
- deduce conclusions on the basis of valid and reliable evidence;
- write up and present a report in accordance with established practices

It is worth noting that, although the majority of dissertations and theses are produced in accordance with the requirements of institutions or examination regulations, the copyright is vested in the author.

Common patterns of presenting material have been developed over a long period of scholarship so that the contents of research reports can easily be assimilated by readers. For instance, reading is made easier by knowing that, whichever dissertation is being looked at, the bibliography will be found in the same place in the body of the text.

Guidance for such preparation of material is plentiful and there are a number of texts that present the reader with a range of information regarding such matters as quoting, bibliographic referencing, table construction and so on.

While such texts are invaluable in explaining the variety of presentational forms acceptable in academic literature, the choice among the alternatives is left to the student writer with the rider that attention must be paid to consistency. This book is intended for students preparing a dissertation or thesis for the first time and for whom making choices from among alternative forms and, at the same time, attempting to be consistent, is often a matter of great concern and frustration.

The purpose of this guide, therefore, is to present a consistent, albeit rigid, pattern which, when strictly followed, will relieve the student of much searching of ways and means and so prevent the dissipation of energies that should be properly directed to the content of the study.

The practices specified here have been culled from a variety of sources, including the recommendations of the British Standards Institute, as being the most useful and practical of the acceptable methods. The guide is presented in two parts.

**Part I Contents** is concerned with the nature, organisation and form of the contents of a dissertation. **Part II Presentation and Style** is concerned with the procedures and practices for producing and presenting a dissertation.

# Part I.
# Contents

# 1. Order of Contents

The content of the whole dissertation includes essential preliminary information and relevant support material in addition to the main body of the text. The order of presentation of the contents is prescribed.

1. Title page

2. Abstract of the Research

3. List of Contents

4. List of Tables

5. List of Figures

6. List of Appendices

7. Glossary of Symbols (for mathematical and scientific researches)

8. Author Declarations

9. Acknowledgements (Preface)

10. Text (Main body of Dissertation)

11. Appendices

12. Bibliography

*Contents*

The List of Contents presents the headings of the chapters and any sub-headings exactly as they appear in the text. It should be noted that the pages preceding the List of Contents are not included in the list.

# 2. Title Page

The information to be given on the Title Page is normally rigidly prescribed by the degree awarding body. Typically, the required information consists of:

   (i)  the full title of the dissertation

  (ii)  the full name of the author and, if desired, any qualifications or distinctions (which should be included in an abbreviated form)

 (iii)  the qualification for which the dissertation is being submitted as part of a statement that it is submitted in partial fulfilment of the requirements of the award.

 (iv)  the degree awarding body

  (v)  the name of the institution in which the research is registered, if different to (iv), the degree awarding body, and that of any collaborating institution

 (vi)  the month and year of submission

(vii)  the number of volumes comprising the dissertation, if more than one.

The layout of the Title Page is centred between the prescribed margins. The vertical centre line is approximately 110mm from the left-hand edge of the page. An example of a Title Page is shown in Figure 2.

AN EMPIRICAL STUDY OF THE PERSONALITY
CHARACTERISTICS OF SOME CHEMISTRY
STUDENTS IN COLLEGES OF FURTHER
EDUCATION

John Brown, B.Sc., P.G.C.E., Adv.Dip.Ed.

Submitted in partial fulfilment of
the requirements for the degree of
MASTER OF PHILOSOPHY

THE UNIVERSITY OF MIDCHESTER
in collaboration with
WESTCHESTER COLLEGE OF FURTHER
EDUCATION

March 1996

**Figure 2.** *Example of a Title Page*

# 3. Abstract

An Abstract of the dissertation is normally required to be bound into each copy of the dissertation and, in addition, it is a frequent requirement for three loose copies to be submitted with the dissertation for examination.

The abstract should not exceed 300 words and be typed single-spaced on one side of A4 paper. The heading of the abstract, which is additional to the 300 words, should give the name of the author and title of the dissertation in capital letters and the year of submission. The margins should be the same as in the body of the text.

Reducing a dissertation to a mere 300 words is often a difficult and demanding task. However, a well written abstract demonstrates the capacity of the author to present the main aspects of an often lengthy study in a coherent and economical form. The abstract, in essence, should provide a brief synopsis of the study by identifying the nature and scope of the work, the major outcomes and the particular contribution it makes to knowledge in the field as shown in the example given in Figure 3. A good abstract should be comprehensive and succinct.

ABSTRACT

JOY STUART                                                    1989

THE DEVELOPMENT AND ASSESSMENT OF CRITICAL
ABILITIES IN ART CRITICISM

The study consisted in the main of a replication of Denise Hickey's (1975) testing of a matrix of the developmental structure of critical abilities, carried out in the USA. The replication study investigated whether Hickey's matrix and assessment were applicable to English education; whether Hickey's research findings and conclusions were valid; and whether replication was an effective method of criticising research methods.

The replication study addressed the problem of the provision of objective measures for critical abilities, and considered whether the development of critical abilities could be associated with intellectual levels and measures of development.

The study was carried out in an English middle school, with a sample of forty subjects, equally divided between subjects aged eleven, and subjects aged thirteen.

The research methodology replicated Hickey's interview format and test procedures. Hickey's measuring instruments provided data for statistical analysis to determine whether the presence of critical abilities could be related to intellectual levels of development. Two diagnostic tests were incorporated into the study to consider the reliability of Hickey's measuring instruments.

The comparability study tended to confirm Hickey's matrix projections, but there were differences between the two pieces of research, which affected the findings and conclusions. The findings were that Hickey's matrix required modification, and that Hickey's assessment procedures were not replaceable. Adaptations to Hickey's matrix were recommended, and an objective measure of critical abilities based on modes of reasoning was devised as an alternative method of determining and assessing the developmental structure of critical abilities. The study also concluded that Hickey's research procedures required revising for a more reliable testing of the matrix and that replication was a sound method of criticising completed research.

The research findings contributed to a fund of knowledge about the development and assessment of critical abilities in relation to intellectual development.

**Figure 3.** *Example of an Abstract*

Dissertations are not normally published, and access to them is invariably limited. Abstracts of research degree dissertations and theses, however, are frequently published in national research databases. Examples of such databases are given below. The abstract, therefore, is important because it can signify whether or not the study is of relevance to a potential reader and, consequently, if it is worth the reader taking the trouble to seek out the complete work so that it could be read in full.

---

Hyams, M (Ed.). (annual). *Aslib Index to Theses*. London: Aslib.

Allison, B (Ed.). (1996). *Allison Research Index of Art and Design*. Second edition. Leicester: ARIAD Associates.

---

# 4. Author Declarations

A dissertation is produced for the exclusive purpose of the award for which it is submitted. To ensure the safeguarding of this academic matter, it is necessary to include in the dissertation a formal statement that the author has not been registered for any other academic award during the period of study and also to state whether any material included in the dissertation has previously been submitted for any other academic awards. An example of the latter might be the inclusion of material in a PhD dissertation that had previously been part of a MPhil study.

It should be added, however, that it is permissible to publish material arising from a study registered for an academic award prior to the submission of the dissertation. Any material published should be referred to in the text and copies of it should be included in the appendices.

As a dissertation is submitted in partial fulfilment of the requirements of an academic award, a statement is included in the Author Declarations that identifies the nature of the advanced studies or research programme of which the dissertation is part.

Author declarations are included in the dissertation immediately after the list of appendices. An example of author declarations is given in Figure 4.

Some universities do not require the author declarations for a dissertation submitted for a higher degree by research to be bound into the dissertation, but to be made separately on a prescribed form. In such cases, three copies of the form are normally required to be submitted along with the dissertation.

AUTHOR DECLARATIONS

1.  During the period of registered study in which this dissertation was prepared the author has not been registered for any other academic award or qualification.
2.  The material included in this dissertation has not been submitted wholly or in part for any academic award or qualification other than that for which it is now submitted.
3.  The programme of advanced study of which this dissertation is part has consisted of:

  (i)  Research Design and Methods course – Years 1 and 2

 (ii)  Participation in Research Colloquia

(iii)  Supervision tutorials
     [All the above were held in the School of Humanities and Social Studies, University of Midchester.]

(iv)  Attendance at relevant research conferences.

J. Brown
March, 1993

**Figure 4.** *Example of Author Declarations*

# 5. Acknowledgements (Preface)

It is customary to acknowledge any assistance or support that has been given during the research. In general literature, Acknowledgements are often included in a section called the Preface, but in dissertations it is customary to use the heading Acknowledgements.

There is no set pattern for acknowledging help and assistance in the work. In general, however, acknowledgements should be brief with an avoidance of flowery language, giving recognition without sentimentality.

Acknowledgement of the contributions and assistance of individuals by name should only be made when such assistance has been of a specific kind, which should be briefly indicated.

> ...and appreciation is due to Dr. J. S. Sweeney, Director of Studies, for his continued support and guidance during the research...
>
> ...and to Mr. K. Brown, M.A., Principal, Westchurch College of Further Education, for advice and assistance in analysing student records...
>
> ...thanks are due to the following heads of colleges and other institutions for cooperation in the testing programme.
> Mr. K. Brown, M.A., Westchester College of Further Education, Leicester.
> Miss D. Curison, B.A., Northfields College, Cardiff.
> Mr. E. Dunn, Southlands Community Centre, Birmingham.
> Mrs. A. Jones...
>
> ...and thanks are due to all the parents and students taking part in the study.

Acknowledgements are contained within the normal side margins of the page, but the top and bottom margins may be adjusted depending on the length of the statement, providing those normal margins are not exceeded.

The Acknowledgements page immediately follows the Author Declarations or, when the Author Declarations are not required to be bound into the dissertation, the List of Appendices.

# 6. Main Body of the Dissertation

The order of some of the contents of the text or main body of the dissertation is firmly established while others depend upon the individual nature of a study. A general guide to the order of presentation of material may be seen as following a logical sequence:

1. Introduction

2. Method of approach or attack

3. Presentation and analysis of evidence

4. Summary and conclusions

How this structure is developed in terms of chapters depends on the nature of the research being reported. However, in general, the flow of the dissertation would be expected to incorporate the following elements.

**Introduction**
A description and explanation of the purposes and scope of the study and the circumstances that led to its formulation.

**Aims of the investigation**
A description of the rationale within which the research questions are to be pursued. The general aims and precise objectives of the research are defined. This section includes a statement of the hypotheses to be examined in the research as well as the assumptions, if any, that underpin the hypotheses.

**The context of the investigation**
A survey, usually historical, of the antecedents of the research and the development of ideas to which the present research

contributes. The theoretical underpinnings of the research are identified and critically appraised. This section normally includes the main survey and critical appraisal of the literature relating to the research topic.

### Research design
A general description of the structure of the research procedures and the methods adopted. This section includes, as appropriate, the choice or development of data collection instruments or tools, the selection of samples, the time scale for the implementation of the research and the means by which collected data are to be analysed. Any pilot studies undertaken in developing the research design are described in full.

### Research implementation
This section describes the means and methods by which the research was pursued in practice, including the organisation and administration of the data-gathering strategies. The steps taken to accumulate the necessary evidence to examine and resolve the research questions are systematically and fully described. The resulting data or evidence are presented and analysed in relation to the hypotheses or research questions.

### Conclusions
The meaning and significance of the analysis of the evidence in relation to the research questions is described and the conclusions clearly presented. The conclusions are examined in the context of the theoretical positions underpinning the research and their implications for practice considered.

### Critical review and reflection
The research is reviewed critically and the strengths and weaknesses of both conception and implementation are identified. This section also presents new questions raised by the research and their potential for future enquiry.

# 7. Appendices

The Appendices section of the dissertation might be thought of as being mainly the repository for the working tools of the investigation and for information that supports the study while not being directly a part of it.

Each dissertation topic requires different kinds of support material, and discretion must be exercised as to the amount of material presented in the appendices. A simple criterion for the inclusion of material lies in the necessity of that material for the comprehension or illumination of the text.

Special pockets can be made in the back cover of the dissertation binding for bulky test material or material that does not lend itself to being bound in with the normal pages. In some cases it may be necessary to have a special box made to carry the appendices. In all such cases, an appropriately headed page describing the contents of each appendix is included in the sequence of appendix pages.

Typical appendices include:

1. Data-collecting instruments used during the investigation, such as tests, questionnaires, observation and interview schedules. It is not necessary to include standardised test material, such as *Raven's Progressive Matrices*, or other National Foundation for Educational Research tests, unless they have been amended in some way.

2. Examples showing how the instruments have been used, such as a completed interview schedule, should be included if their inclusion helps the reader to understand the work methods.

3. Raw data, particularly if there is a lot of it, rarely finds its way into the main body of the dissertation as it is the analysis and interpretation of data that carries meaning. However, sometimes such data are a necessary support for the text and would be included as an Appendix. Complex or lengthy tables or figures might be included as Appendices either because they would interrupt the flow of the text unnecessarily or because the text includes abstracts or summaries of them. For instance, tables in the text might show the totals or a breakdown of the complete tables that are presented as Appendices.

4. It is normally necessary for computer software developed as part of the research to be submitted as part of the dissertation and this would be included as an appendix. If the full listing of programmes is too bulky to be submitted in hard copy, it may be included in the dissertation on microfiche or computer disk.

5. When the main body of the research results in practical work that is exhibited in some form, it is normally required for a permanent record in a photographic or other form to be submitted with the dissertation. A complete record of such work would constitute an Appendix.

6. Some dissertations employ a wide range of technical terms with specialised meanings or applications within the context of the research. A glossary of technical terms used in the dissertation, therefore, would be included appropriately as an appendix. A glossary of mathematical or scientific symbols, however, is not presented as an appendix but is sited in the preliminary pages as noted earlier in the Order of Contents (p.19).

7. Colloquial language used in response to particularly searching questions in, for instance, an interview, often gives colour to the interpretation of the opinions expressed. Such verbatim responses or transcripts of tape

recordings might be appropriately included in the appendices.

8. Long extracts from official documents such as White Papers, Examination Council requirements, speeches and so on, may be included as appendices when it is necessary to the comprehension of the text for the reader to have them available at first hand.

9. Lists of equipment used or observed, lists of schools, firms, laboratories or other institutions visited or reviewed, and other such relevant collations would form appendices.

Appendices are numbered sequentially with upper case roman numerals (eg I; II; III; IV). Each appendix should have a heading that states precisely and concisely what the appendix contains. Both the appendix number and heading are capitalised and, if longer than one line, single-line spaced.

---

APPENDIX III. AN EXAMPLE OF CONSTRUCTING A
THEORETICAL MODEL.

APPENDIX XII. TESTS USED FOR THE ASSESSMENT OF
SPATIAL ABILITY.
a) VISUALISATION TEST b) CARDBOARD MODEL GAME

---

The List of Appendices presents the headings as they appear on the Appendices themselves.

# 8. Bibliography

The Bibliography includes texts and all other sources that have been referred to in the body of the dissertation. It does not include peripheral or background reading. The bibliography is the final section of the dissertation and is located after the appendices. Bibliographies at the end of chapters are unnecessary.

## Bibliographical references

In order to identify a particular text clearly and accurately, it is necessary to have certain minimal reference information. This information primarily consists of:

- the name of the author;
- the year of publication;
- the title of the publication;
- the place of publication;
- the name of the publisher.

Further detail is dependent upon the nature of the publication being referred to. While there is more than one standard way of presenting this bibliographical data, it is important that consistency in referencing is maintained by keeping to one system. The system described here is generally known as the 'Harvard system' and although it appears to be complicated it is remarkably simple to use once the habit of applying it has been acquired. The following examples illustrate the use of capital and lower case letters, italicisation, punctuation marks and layout, all of which have a specific function. In manuscript form or in typescript, underlining is used to indicate typographical *italics*.

## Editions

The simplest reference form is that for books that have been
published as single editions.

---

Arnheim, R. (1956). *Art Education: Its Philosophy and
Psychology*. Indianapolis: Bobbs Merrill.

Graham, R. (1966). *The Pickworth Fragment*. Wymondham:
Wymondham Press.

---

When books have been published in subsequent editions it is
important to specify the edition number as there are often
considerable differences between editions. The edition
number is shown in parentheses after the title.

---

Hall, L. (1979). *Business Administration* (3rd edit.). Estover,
Plymouth: Macdonald and Evans.

Lowenfeld, V. and Brittain, L. (1970). *Creative and Mental
Growth* (5th edit.). New York: Collier Macmillan.

---

## Collected works

Publications that consist of collections of writings by a
number of authors are identified under the names of the
editors. Listings, indexes or collections of abstracts are similarly identified by the names of editors. The editors are designated by the abbreviations (Ed.) or (Eds.) after the name.

---

Weinshall, T. D. (Ed.). (1977). *Culture and Management*.
Harmondsworth: Penguin.

Eisner, E.W. and Ecker, D.W. (Eds.). (1966). *Readings in Art
Education*. London: Ginn Blaisdell.

---

References to specific chapters or articles in edited collections are identified under the names of the particular authors and then reference is made to the whole publication as above.

If the date when the specific chapter was originally published differs from that of the collected edition it is necessary to include both dates.

It is standard practice to give the page numbers of the article and, as the whole publication is the primary source of reference, it is the title of the whole publication that is italicised or underlined to indicate italics.

---

Fayerweather, J. (1960). Personal Relations. *In* Weinshall, T.D. (Ed.) (1977). *Culture and Management.* Harmondsworth: Penguin. 107–135.

Kaufman, I. (1971). The Art of Curriculum Making in the Arts. *In* Eisner, E.W. (Ed.). *Confronting Curriculum Reform.* Boston: Little Brown and Co. 91–112.

---

### Articles in periodicals

Articles in periodicals are always the most difficult to locate so it is essential to have complete bibliographical data. The actual periodical in which an article appears is the major reference source and so it is the name of the periodical that is italicised or underlined. Most learned journals tend to have long titles and so for bibliographic purposes these are reduced to standardised abbreviations. Periodicals differ in the ways in which the different issues are designated but the most popular form is the attribution of a volume number, which quite often relates to a particular year of publication, and then an issue or part number within a volume. The numbers of the pages on which the article appears are also given.

> Feldman, E. B. (1973). The Teacher as Model Critic. *J. Aesth. Educ.* 7, 1, 50–58.
> In this example the article is in Volume 7, Part 1 of the *Journal of Aesthetic Education* on pages 50 to 58.
>
> Hannigan, J. A. (1980). Fragmentation in Science: The Case of Futurology. *Sociology. Rev.* 28, 2, 317–32.

## Unpublished material

Material that has not been published in the senses described above, such as theses or dissertations submitted for academic qualifications or papers read at conferences, is identified by the name and nature of the material as well as the source or location.

> Graham, R. (1974). *The Casquets*. Unpublished paper. Second Annual Morison Lecture. Manchester Polytechnic.
>
> Hancocks, M. (1973). *Creativity in Education – A Selective Review*. Unpublished M.Sc. thesis, University of Bradford.

## Non-English texts

Texts and other materials written in languages other than English are given the appropriate bibliographical reference in the language of origin but a translation of the title is included in parentheses after the title itself. The parenthesised title is not italicised.

> Adorno, T. W. (1970). *Teoria Estetica* (Aesthetic Theory). Lisboa: Edico-es 70.

The references for texts written in languages that use characters other than those in the Roman alphabet, such as Russian or Japanese, are given in the full English translation.

## Non-authored texts

References are normally identified in the text of the dissertation and listed in the bibliography under the name of author or authors. However, some texts or other works, such as reference books and journals, do not have a specific author and are not able to be referenced in the standard format. In these cases, the texts are referenced using the title as the identifier, in place of the author's name. When reference is made to a particular issue of a journal, the year of publication is given along with the volume and issue number.

---

*Collins English Dictionary* (3rd edition). (1991). Glasgow: HarperCollins Publishers.

*Hypertalk Beginner's Guide: An Introduction to Scripting* (1989). Cupertino, CA: Apple Computer, Inc.

*Journal of Art and Design Education* 15, 2. (1996). Oxford: Blackwell Publishers.

---

References in the text of the dissertation to non-authored texts are made, similarly, using the title, or the first two or three words of the title, as the identifier, along with the date of publication and page number(s).

---

...whereas a 'dissertation' has been defined as 'a written thesis, often based on original research, usually required for a higher degree' (*Collins English Dictionary*, 1991, p.454).

The Hypertalk words constitute a scripting language (*Hypertalk Beginner's Guide*, 1989, p.24).

---

## Non-print media
References to texts or other material available in non-print media follow the same format as print-based publications. The medium and other identifiers are specified within the reference.

---

Macdonald, H. (Director) (1996). *Beautiful Thing*. (Film). Iverheath, UK: Pinewood Studios and Channel 4.

Conley, R. (1992). *Rosemary Conley's Whole Body Programme 2*. (Videotape). London: BBC.

Erhard, W. (1985). *Effective action and accomplishment*. (Audio Cassette Recording). San Francisco, CA.: Audiotapes.

---

## Electronic media
References to material transmitted or available electronically, such as computer programmes, CD-ROM, the Internet and e-mail, follow the same format as print-based materials but with minor variations. In all cases, specific identifiers should be included in the sequence to show access routes.

### *Computer programmes*
Computer programmes that have been used in the research or have been referred to as data sources need to be identified either as an authored text or by the name of the programme.

---

*Data Mate Survey Software* (1995) Worcester: Simple Surveys.

---

### *CD-ROM*
Material published on CD-ROM, whether reference works or interactive programmes, is referenced in the same form as non-book media.

> MacRae, S (1995). *Introduction to Research Design and Statistics*. (CD-ROM). Leicester: British Psychological Society.

## Internet

References to articles and other material accessible online via FTP (File Transfer Protocol), WWW (World Wide Web), or Telnet Sites must specify the pathway for access. Sites may not be permanent and so the date the site was visited needs to be given. It is of interest to note that the symbol ~ in a reference indicates that the site is a personal site.

> Frantz, G. D. and McConnell. S. K. (1966). Restriction of Late Cerebral Cortex Progenitors to an Upper Layer Fate. *Neuron*, 17, 1, 55–61.
> http://www.cell.com/neuron/abstract/j0437.html (24 June 1996)
>
> Li, X. and Crane, N. (1995). *Bibliographic Formats for Citing Electronic Information*.
> http://www.uvm.edu/~xli/reference/estyles.html. (15 July 1996).

## E-mail

Articles or other texts sent to subscribers via an e-mail List-serv, including journals published electronically, should indicate the access route and procedure to be followed to gain access. The date the message was received needs to be given.

> Worden, S. (1996). *Networking in art and design* (Summary). Design-Research@mailbase.ac.uk. (24 July 1996.) Available e-mail: mailbase@ac.uk. Message: 'Subscribe Design-Research'

# Bibliography Compilation

When compiling sources of reference into a bibliography the entries are listed in alphabetical order of the names of the authors. If reference is made to more than one work by the same author the entries are listed in chronological order of the dates of publication. When reference is made to more than one work by an author, all of which were published in the same year, the works are differentiated by appending the letters a, b, c and so on to the year of publication, as in (1974a); (1974b); (1974c). References to the specific texts within the dissertation must, of course, be the same as in the Bibliography.

Compiling a bibliography can be a tedious task and it can also be frustrating when, for example, new references need to be slotted into a partially compiled bibliography. Some problems can be obviated if, throughout the research, a record of each reference is kept which is accurate and complete and in the form in which it will appear in the bibliography. It is also helpful to have a workable system for organising the records, such as on index cards that can be sorted and stacked. Even more helpful is a computer database programme, which can be added to as necessary, and which, when required, can sort and print out the entire bibliography ready for inclusion in the dissertation. In all cases, it is wise not to have the bibliography typed in its final form until after the whole dissertation has been completed.

Bibliographical entries are typed single spaced. In order to make the entries in a bibliography clearly identifiable, the second and subsequent lines of each entry are indented, and double spaces are left between entries.

Adorno, T. W. (1970). *Teoria Estetica* (Aesthetic Theory). Lisboa: Edico-es 70.

Anderson, D. M. (1961). *Elements of Design.* New York: Holt, Rinehart and Winston.

Arnheim, R. (1966). *Towards a Psychology of Art.* London: Faber and Faber.

Arnheim, R. (1970). *Visual Thinking.* London: Faber and Faber.

British Standards Institute (1990). *Recommendations for the presentation of theses and dissertations.* BS 4821. London: British Standards Institute.

Douglas, J. M. B., Ross, J. M., and Samson, H. R. (1968). *All our Future.* London: Davies.

Erhard, W. (1985). *Effective action and accomplishment.* (Audio Cassette Recording). San Francisco, CA.: Audiotapes.

Fayerweather, J. (1960) Personal Relations. *In* Weinshall, T. D. (Ed.) (1977). *Culture and Management.* Harmondsworth: Penguin. 107–135.

Feldman, E. B. (1973). The Teacher as Model Critic. *J. Aesth. Educ.* 7, 1, 50–58.

Graham, R. (1974a). The Foulis Archive Press. *Private Library.* Second Series, 7, 1, 33.

Graham, R. (1974b). Letter from Glasgow. *Amer. Notes and Queries.* XII, 8, 125–6.

Hall, L. (1979). *Business Administration* (3rd edit.). Estover, Plymouth: Macdonald and Evans.

Hyams, M (Ed.). (annual). *Aslib Index to Theses.* London: Aslib.

Li, X. and Crane, N. (1995). *Bibliographic Formats for Citing Electronic Information.* http://www.uvm.edu/~xli/reference/estyles.html. (15 July 1996).

Weinshall, R. D. (1977). *Culture and Management.* Harmondsworth: Penguin.

Worden, S. (1996). *Networking in art and design (Summary).* Design-Research@mailbase.ac.uk. (24 July 1996.) Available e-mail: mailbase@ac.uk. Message: 'Subscribe Design-Research'

**Figure 5.** *Example of a Bibliography*

# Part II.
# Presentation and Style

# 9. Page Size

The size of paper normally used for dissertations is known as A4 (210 mm x 297 mm) and is used vertically (sometimes referred to as 'portrait'). The paper should be of good quality and with sufficient opacity to ensure the type does not show through. Only one side of the paper is used.

Occasionally, an item to be included either in the text or as an appendix, such as a table or a diagram, which cannot be reduced, requires a page size larger than A4. While maintaining the normal vertical dimension, the paper may be folded as shown in Figure 6. To avoid being cut during the binding stage of the dissertation, the fold must not be more than 195mm from the left-hand edge of the paper. Similarly, the folded section edge should not be less than 40mm from the left-hand edge of the paper to avoid being sewn in.

**Figure 6.** *Example of an oversized page*

# 10. Page Margins

Page margins allow for the sewing and trimming during the binding of the dissertation. The visual appearance of the page is also dependent upon the proportion of the text area to margin area.

Margins must be consistent throughout the dissertation. The most appropriate margins for the A4 paper size are:

    (i)  Top and right-hand margins       20mm
   (ii)  Left-hand margins (the spine of the book)  40mm
  (iii)  Bottom margins            40mm

Pages with exceptions to these margins:

- Title page – see Example of a Title Page, p.22;
- Acknowledgements – see acknowledgements, p.28;
- Chapter pages – the first page of each chapter is given a top margin of 40mm;
- Pages that include tables or figures of unusual sizes – see p.47.

# 11. Page Numbers

Pages are numbered consecutively throughout the whole of the dissertation. Pages are given arabic numerals. *Page numbers* are placed 20mm from the bottom of the page and are centred between the margin lines (110mm from left-hand edge of the paper).

The exception to this rule is the title page which, although technically designated page 1, is not actually numbered. Appendices (such as off-prints of articles) that have been previously page-numbered in their publications, are re-numbered within the sequence in which they are presented in the dissertation.

As the order of the different sections of the dissertation may be changed while the work and the typing or word-processing of the work progresses, the final numbering of the pages should be left until the entire dissertation is assembled. If typing the page numbers in at this stage presents great difficulties, it is sometimes permissible, with the prior agreement of the supervisor, to write the page numbers in ink, provided they are neat and unobtrusive. This concession does not apply normally to research degree theses or dissertations in which page numbers must be typed. To keep the dissertation in order during its assemblage, it is helpful to number the pages temporarily in pencil.

# 12. Style of Writing

Dissertations are written in the English language except in very unusual circumstances for which the examining bodies provide specific regulations.

The use of a consistent and appropriate style of writing is an important part of the whole research procedure. Thorough and valuable research findings are of little use unless they are clearly and effectively communicated.

The purpose of a dissertation is to present the products of a serious study in a clear, dispassionate manner. It should not be the intention of the writer to be amusing, entertaining or even to persuade the reader to a particular point of view. The main objective is to present the procedures and findings of a systematic enquiry which, for example, might include a hypothesis, the background of ideas from which the hypothesis was derived, the factual data collected, the resultant acceptance or rejection of the hypothesis on the basis of the evidence and an exposition of the consequences of such findings. The emphasis should be on a clear, logical and objective presentation of material with a sharp analysis of the evidence, although this need be neither dull nor pedantic.

It is important to bear in mind the potential readers of the dissertation. As most dissertation topics lie in highly specialised fields, the readers are likely to be experts within those fields. As was noted in the Introduction to this book, the initial readers are likely to be the examiners or assessors of the dissertation. Reading at this level is, of necessity, highly critical and any flaws in reasoning, for instance, or the presentation of unsupported assertions and unqualified assumptions would be quickly noted and, in consequence, the import of the whole study might suffer.

Although the social sciences do not have the constancy of the physical sciences, replication of the whole or parts of research projects is common and is often necessary. Such replication is only possible if the description of the research is **clear** and **complete**. Ambiguity of any kind not only invalidates the possibility of replication but is an indication of imprecision of thought on the part of the writer.

The dissertation can be seen as a logical ordering of a chain of ideas, data, analyses and interpretations. Disordered material reveals little more than that the writer has not understood the relevance of the material he/she is presenting. The grouping and regrouping of ideas and data into logical sequences is a major part of the intellectual effort that dissertation writing demands.

Every writer develops his/her own methods of organising material, but there is a fairly general pattern. At an early stage a draft outline of the whole work should be drawn up with the expectation that, as the work proceeds, it may undergo frequent revision and extension. The advantage of such an outline, or map of intended or actual development, is that omissions, illogical orderings or questionable emphases can be detected while the work is still in a malleable form. The intention here should be directed towards systematic and disciplined work methods.

Although a completed dissertation or thesis is presented as a coherent, sequential ordering of aims, procedures and outcomes, it is rarely written by starting on page one and continuing through to the end. It is usual for the constituent parts to be written, refined and rewritten several times. Revising the order in which the parts are to be presented often requires other adjustments to be made. Furthermore, as the introduction is intended to illuminate the reader as to what to expect in the dissertation, it is usual for the final draft of the introduction to be written when all other parts of the dissertation have been completed.

It will be found valuable to give each section a precise heading, showing a clear indication of the content of that section. Indeed, each paragraph should be sufficiently self-contained in terms of ideas as to be similarly labelled, although these would not necessarily be included in the final dissertation. When preparing headings, a similar grammatical structure and capitalisation should be adhered to.

---

4. Controllability
      4.1 Intentions of the Cognitive Dimension
      4.2 Intentions of the Affective Dimension
      4.3 Intentions of the Pragmatic Dimension

---

The inclusion of non-literal elements, such as formulae, is necessary in many dissertations, particularly in the fields of mathematics and science. In order to identify formulae in sequence, they are designated numerically within the divisions or sub-divisions of the sections of the text in which they occur.

$$G_N(s,t) = \left( \frac{\alpha(t) + [1 - \alpha(t) - \beta(t)]S}{1 - \beta(t)S} \right)^{n_0} \qquad (7.15)$$

It should be remembered that the purpose of the dissertation is to present a precise and lucid account of an investigation rather than use the work as a vehicle for the demonstration of masterly rhetoric. A simple, straightforward style of writing is infinitely preferable to the use of long, involved sentences filled with technical jargon. Care should be taken to avoid using a particular term in one sense in one place in the text and in a different sense in others. Any new or unfamiliar terms used in the text should be defined or used in such a way that the meanings are made clear.

    Tenses should be consistent throughout and, as the dissertation is, for the most part, a record of past events, the reportage is carried out in the **past** tense. The logic of this can be clearly seen. The **present** tense is used only when referring the reader to tables or figures in the text or other parts of the dissertation.

As a research report demands a formal rather than colloquial style of writing, the **third** person is adhered to throughout. Personal pronouns (ie I, me, we, you, us) are not used. The only exception to this rule is in reporting 'naturalistic' or 'qualitative' research, which may take the form of a diary style of writing. Although the skill of writing in the third person seems difficult to acquire, most people are able to do so with some perseverance. Attempts to evade this requirement by the use of such ploys as 'The writer observed...' or 'One felt that...' should be avoided.

Spelling mistakes are unacceptable in dissertations as are grammatical errors. A dictionary should be used to check any other than simple, straightforward words. Simplified spellings such as 'thro' or 'phone' are not used in dissertations. A thesaurus helps considerably to avoid the repetitious use of phrases. While the dissertation is still at the draft stage it is worthwhile asking a lay reader to check through it for spelling, punctuation and grammatical errors. Users of word-processing computer programmes should use the programme's 'spell check' or similar facility, if one is available. This should be done before it is submitted for professional reading.

Authors for whom English is not their first or native language, no matter how fluent they believe themselves to be in the use of English, should always ask a native colloquial English speaker to read through their work before submitting it to a research supervisor. This is not only to ensure that it is grammatically sound but also to tease out, discuss and clarify issues or meanings that might otherwise read as being ambiguous or confused. As writing in a second language is almost always difficult, some institutions permit students to write their dissertations in their own language and then employ a professional translator to produce the work in English. In such cases, care should be taken to ensure that the translator is familiar with the subject field. It is worth noting that any oral examination of the dissertation is invariably conducted in English.

# 13. Abbreviations

Many institutions, national bodies, academic awards and so on are commonly known by their acronyms or the initials of the full title. While such acronyms or abbreviations are acceptable within the text of the dissertation, the name or title is written out in full the first time it occurs so that it is properly identified.

> ...within the regulations of the Council for National Academic Awards for the approval of examiners for the Doctor of Philosophy degree. While the C.N.A.A. recognised that the examination of Ph.D. candidates...

Abbreviations other than those referred to above are not normally employed in the main body of the text. Commonly used abbreviations such as those below may, however, be used in bibliographic references, footnotes, tables, appendices and the bibliography. The same applies to the use of symbols and so, for instance, the term 'per cent' would be used in the text whilst the symbol '%' may be used in the tables.

## Common Abbreviations

| | |
|---|---|
| anon | anonymous |
| Bk., Bks. | book(s) |
| c. | *circa* – about (approximate date, eg c.1623) |
| Chap., Chaps. | chapter(s) |
| col., cols. | column(s) |
| e.g. | *exempli gratia* – for example |

| | |
|---|---|
| edit. edits. | edition(s) |
| Ed., Eds., | editor(s) |
| *et al.* | *et alii* – and others. May be used in the text for subsequent reference to a work with multiple authors after the full reference has first been made. eg Witkin *et al.,* 1954. |
| ibid. | *ibidem* – in the same book |
| i.e. | *id est* – that is (to say) |
| MS., MSS. | manuscript(s) |
| n., nn. | footnote(s) |
| n.d. | no date – when the date of publication is not known |
| n.n. | no name – when either the author or publisher is not known |
| n.p. | no place – when the location of the publisher is not known |
| op. cit. | *opere citato* – in the work already quoted |
| No., Nos. | Number(s) |
| p., pp. | page(s) |
| para., paras. | paragraph(s) |
| Pt., Pts. | part(s) |
| rev. | revised, revision |
| Sec., Secs. | section(s) |
| trans. | translated by |
| Vol., Vols. | volume(s) |
| vs., vss. | verse(s) |

If any other than common abbreviations are used in the dissertation, a key should be provided. This should be placed after the list of appendices.

# 14. Numbers

When *numbers* are to be included in the prose of the text, numbers less than one hundred, round numbers and numbers at the beginning of sentences are spelled out in full. Fractions are also spelled out unless they form part of a larger number. Numbers in sequence are presented as numerals.

---

One hundred and forty students took part in the experiment, three-quarters of whom were designated as haptic. The responses to Questions 83, 107, 192 and 204 of the questionnaire showed that 121 students considered...

...the effects of the Revised Code of 1861 were greatly diminished by the end of the nineteenth century.

...and of these, forty-two people considered that...

---

The exceptions to this rule are in referring to chapters, tables, figures or appendices in the present dissertation when the designated numerals are used.

---

As was shown in Chapter 3 and in the observations presented in Appendix IV, the process...

---

# 15. Chapters

Chapters constitute the major way of organising the whole content of a dissertation. Each chapter, however, represents the bringing together of ideas, data or other information relating to a central idea. Although chapters vary in length and complexity, the main issues in each chapter should be clearly evident. It is recommended good practice to include a short summary at the end of each chapter outlining the major points covered and conclusions reached in the chapter. This is not only very helpful to the reader but it also serves to demonstrate the author's grasp of the material.

The material within a single chapter may lend itself to being sub-divided into cohesive units. As indicated in the section on style of writing (p.50), sub-divisions of chapters should be given headings that clearly describe the content. Sub-headings should be consistent in form and for clarity can be identified by using the decimal system of numbering (4.1; 4.2; 4.3; etc.). Further sub-divisions are numbered by extending the decimals (4.3.1; 4.3.2; 4.3.3.; etc.). Formulae are numbered by extending the decimals. (4.3.3.2).

The chapter heading should state succinctly the main area of concern of the chapter. Chapters are numbered consecutively throughout the text with arabic numerals. Two line spaces are allowed between the chapter number and the heading which, if longer than one line, is single-line spaced. Both chapter number and heading are capitalised.

---

CHAPTER 6

MOTIVATIONAL FACTORS AFFECTING THE
ACHIEVEMENT OF CHEMISTRY STUDENTS

---

Chapter sub-headings are numbered consistently through-out the chapter and are not capitalised.

---

6.1 Personality and other background factors

---

Chapter headings and main sub-headings are included in the List of Contents exactly as they appear in the text.

# 16. References

Comprehensive reference to relevant work of other authors is an essential part of research presentation. Such reference indicates the author's knowledge of the field in which the research is located and is also used to provide an appropriate context for matters arising in the research itself.

References to the work of others need to be made with discretion. It is important that all references are directly relevant and pertinent to the research project and are not included simply to demonstrate the breadth and extent of the author's reading.

References are primarily included as evidence relating to or supporting points, issues, trends and so on, that have been identified by the author. This function should be evident in the way references are made.

There are a number of ways of making specific reference to the work of other writers. It is self-evident that, as full information on every source is included in the bibliography, it is only necessary to identify each reference so that it can be found in the bibliography.

As a rule it is unnecessary and inappropriate to include any information in the text that can be found elsewhere in the dissertation, as would be the case in the following example:

'...whilst Sir Cyril Burt pointed out in "Mental and Scholastic Tests", published in England in 1921, that...'. All that is required in the text is the author's surname and the date of publication of the reference. However, there are several ways in which references can be made.

1. When the author is being referred to within a sentence construction, only the surname is used and the date of publication is parenthesised.

> While Burt (1921) pointed out that…

2.  Reference can be made without actually including the author in the construction of the sentence.

> …an early attempt at formulating a stage theory (Burt, 1921) may be seen as a precursor to…

3.  When reference is made to more than one author, authors and dates of publication succeed each other in chronological order within the parentheses, and are separated by semi-colons:

> …and some attempts at developing stages (Kerschensteiner, 1905; Burt, 1921; Lowenfeld, 1964) may be seen…

4.  When the flow of the text is uncomfortably interrupted by making references in this way, the reference may be made at the end of the sentence or paragraph providing the direct connection can be recognised.

> …although earlier attempts at developing stages did not make this apparent (Burt, 1921). Recently there…

5.  Occasionally, when a specific point has been made by an author it is necessary to inform the reader of the exact page in the text where the point was made. In this case, the page number follows the date within the parentheses.

> ...in discussing the role of the imagination, the point made by
> Arnheim (1956, p.114) that...

6. When reference is made within the text to a work by two authors, the names of both authors are given. If the reference is parenthesised to identify a particular point or quotation, the 'and' is replaced by an ampersand (&). For example, '...Frantz and McConnell (1966)...' would be used within a sentence but '...(Frantz & McConnell, 1966)...' would be used as an identification.

7. When the reference is to the work of three or more authors, the names of all the authors are given in the first reference to the work but subsequently only the name of the first author is given along with the abbreviation *et al.* or et al. to indicate other authors.

For example, '...Douglas, Ross and Simpson (1968)...' would be a first reference while subsequent references would be '...Douglas *et al.* (1968)...' or '...(Douglas *et al*, 1968)...' if used as an identification.

8. References to organisations or bodies with recognised acronyms or initials are made using the full title for the first reference to the work but subsequently the acronym or initials may be used.

For example, '...Department of Education and Science (1973)...' would be the first reference while subsequent references would be '...D.E.S. (1973)...'.
Some organisations, such as Unesco, use the acronym as the official name but it is only in such cases that the initials are not punctuated with periods or full stops.

# 17. Notes

Notes additional to the main body of the text should be avoided whenever possible. However, they are sometimes included in dissertations and can be presented as footnotes relating to matters on a particular page, chapter notes relating to matters in each chapter or dissertation notes referring to matters throughout the whole main body of the text.

Notes are used for various purposes but, principally, they are intended to provide additional information at particular points without interrupting the main flow of the text. These may be used to illuminate issues raised in the text; to develop or illustrate arguments; to explain particular points in detail; or to give bibliographic references.

However, as indicated above, notes should be avoided unless they are felt to be essential as, more often than not, they defeat their own purpose. Notes tend to make the reading of the dissertation difficult and it is often irritating to the reader to have to leave the flow of the text in order to find and then read the notes. This is particularly the case with chapter or dissertation notes but it also applies even when the notes are on the same page, as with footnotes. Furthermore, the inclusion of the note number in the text, either as a raised number or a parenthesised number, leads to typographic difficulty and, in the case of footnotes, there are problems in judging and balancing the number of lines on the page taken up by the body of the text and the number of lines to be left for the footnotes. However, some word processor programmes make provision for this. When included, all notes are typed single line spaced with a double line space between notes. Notes must be kept within the standard page margins.

## Footnotes

Footnotes are numbered sequentially in arabic numbers on the page on which they appear. Three line spaces are left between the bottom line of the text and the first line of the footnotes.

## Chapter Notes

Chapter notes are numbered sequentially in arabic numbers within each chapter. Chapter notes are placed at the end of the chapter and begin on the page after the last page of text.

## Dissertation Notes

Dissertation notes are numbered sequentially in arabic numbers throughout the main body of the text. Dissertation notes are included as a free-standing section of the dissertation and are located after the final chapter and before the appendices.

# 18. Quotations

It should be accepted as a general principle that direct quotations are to be kept to a minimum as, for the most part, the writer's interpretation of what has been read is more important than merely presenting the reader with a compilation of other people's words. Numerous direct quotations make dull, interrupted reading and often are an indication of the writer's inability to assimilate what he/she has read into his/her own thinking. However, occasionally it happens that only an author's exact words will illustrate the point being made or it may be that an author has used words in a particular or personal way. The use of a term such as 'visual thinking' would be a good example of this latter point. It should go without saying that any quotations included in the text must be absolutely accurate and a clear indication given if any words are left out or any other alterations made. Any unusual or wrong spellings in the original quotation must be included unaltered but identified by being followed immediately by the term (sic). The term (sic) is always placed in parentheses to indicate that it has been inserted in the quotation. All quotations must be identified by giving the full reference information including the page number.

There are two ways of quoting:

1. Short quotations of not more than, say, twelve words may be included in the normal flow of the text and are identified by using *single* quotation marks.

...yet Logan (1965, p.65) stated that secondary art education 'is ready to reach more people of greater ultimate diversity' and then he described such effort as 'most worthwhile'. This attitude...

...although the validity of such a notion as that of the 'child behaving as an artist' (Barkan, 1955, p.87) may be questioned. In relation to this point, Barkan suggested that the child's 'overt behavior' (sic) may be...

Quotations within short quotations included in the flow of the text are identified by *double* quotation marks.

...while Loree and Koch (1960, p.154) reported results confirming the hypothesis that competencies 'could be considerably improved by simulating "immediate" reward conditions'...

2. Long quotations are *indented* and *single-spaced* so that they are immediately apparent to the reader. Quotation marks are not required. The exact page number must be indicated at the end of the quotation.

...the assertion by Burt (1921) that the child

   ...is trying, by his pictures, to communicate, or perhaps merely to express, and sometimes only, it would seem, to catalogue, all that he remembers, or all that interests him, in the subject to be drawn. (p.349).

The child, Burt suggested, draws...

Quotations within long, indented quotations are identified by single quotation marks.

> An institutional law violation is a violation of the rules of the school, such as: 'talk when you're supposed to study', 'not take your seat when the bell rings'. (Smith, 1986, p.743).

# 19. Tables

A Table can be considered a complete statistical statement and, in a sense, should be able to exist separate from the text. A table should not need a lengthy explanation on how it is to be interpreted. A well-organised and presented table should be self-explanatory, simple and coherent and bring together a number of related facts to illustrate a single important idea, fact or finding. The purpose of a table is to present statistical data clearly and economically in a way that helps the reader to see relationships, appreciate meaningfulness of proportions or assess significances in the data more easily than a prose explanation would be able to do.

A table is always placed after the first reference to it in the text, usually at the end of the paragraph. If it is not possible to fit the table on the same page as the reference, it is placed at the end of the first paragraph on the following page.

Tables should be kept within the normal page margins. Tables that are longer than one half of the vertical margins are centred on pages of their own. Tables longer than a page can be continued on the next page and, in this case, the table and column headings are repeated exactly on the second page. On the rare occasion that a table is too wide to be presented vertically on the page, it may be placed on its side on the page to read from the spine down. In this case, care should be taken to ensure that the margin at the top of the table is the measurement for the left hand margin (40mm).

It is important that all descriptions of data within a table are accurate and complete although brief. The style should be consistent throughout and, within any one table, the grammatical structure should be the same. Long column headings may be typed broadside to read from the bottom to the top of the page. Abbreviations should be kept to a minimum (see abbreviations, p.54).

Lines or rules in tables are necessary only insofar as they help to group data in specific ways. Row and column headings are usually separated from the statistics by rules, for instance, as are totals. Side rules are not necessary.

The table heading should state precisely the content of the table. Tables are given arabic numerals, which run sequentially throughout the dissertation. Two spaces are allowed between the table number and the heading, which are both typed in capitals. If the heading is longer than one line it is single spaced.

Tables are referred to in the text by their allocated numbers. For example, '...as shown in Table 9' is used and not '...as shown in the following table'.

TABLE 9

INTERCORRELATIONS OF BACKGROUND VARIABLES (IN THE DIAGONAL, INTERJUDGE CORRELATIONS CORRECTED BY THE SPEARMAN-BROWN FORMULA) AND RELATION TO AESTHETIC JUDGEMENT

|  | 1 | 2 | 3 | 4 | Aesthetic judgement | N |
|---|---|---|---|---|---|---|
| 1. Education in art | 0.89 | 0.57 | 0.42 | 0.22 | 0.49** | 138 |
| 2. Experience in galleries |  | 0.89 | 0.46 | 0.36 | 0.49** | 138 |
| 3. Art-related hobbies |  |  | 0.86 | 0.26 | 0.21* | 126 |
| 4. Family attitude toward art |  |  |  | 0.88 | 0.18* | 132 |

* p< .05; ** p< .0l

Tables of correlations may be reduced in size by omitting the zeros and decimal points provided that a note 'Decimal points omitted' is made at the bottom of the table.

Tables that are borrowed from another source or publication are classed in the dissertation as figures and are not numbered within the table sequence. In this case, the reference for the source of the table is included immediately below the table.

Source: McManus (1991, p.48).

The List of Tables presents the headings as they appear on the tables in the text.

# 20. Figures

It should be remembered throughout the dissertation that the major aim is to present data, ideas and information by the most appropriate, economical and efficient means. A diagram or map, for instance, might present a relationship or point of view that would otherwise take up several pages of verbal description. A graph or histogram might demonstrate visually a trend that would otherwise be difficult to present. Examples of art work or other pictorial material, for instance, that was produced or used in the investigation may be necessary to illustrate the text and these may be reproduced photographically. Included as figures would be maps, diagrams, histograms, graphs, photographs, tables that have been borrowed from another source or publication and any other illustrative material. Colour may be used in figures provided its purpose is to add to the clarity of meaning and is not for the sake of decoration.

Figures always follow, and never precede, the first reference to them in the text, normally at the end of the paragraph in which the reference has been made. If the remaining space on that page does not allow this, the figure should be placed at the end of the first paragraph on the next page.

A figure whose vertical dimension is more than half that of the typed area should be placed on a page by itself.

## Figure Sizes

(i) Figures should not exceed the normal page margins.

(ii) If the figure is narrower than the margins it is placed centrally between the margins.

(iii) If it is not possible by photographic or other means to reduce a large figure to normal margin size, it may be folded as outlined in the section on page size (p.47).

(iv) When two or more figures are being included on the same page, as for instance in photographic reproductions, they should be placed symmetrically either vertically or horizontally.

The figure heading should state precisely what the figure seeks to demonstrate. Headings longer than one line are single spaced. Figures are given arabic numerals which run consecutively throughout the text. Two line spaces are allowed between the figure number and the heading, which are both typed in capital letters.

In the case of illustrations, such as diagrams, photographs or photographic reproductions, the heading may be placed below the figure on the same line as the figure number.

As with tables, figures are referred to in the text by their designated numbers, for example, '...as may be seen in Figure 23...'

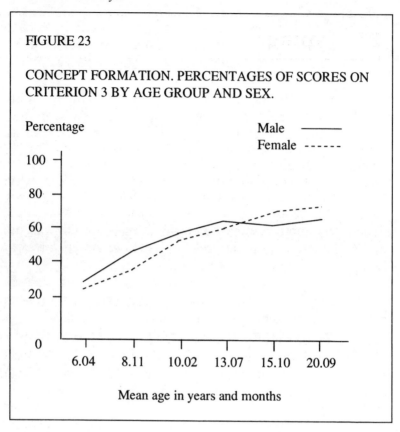

FIGURE 23

CONCEPT FORMATION. PERCENTAGES OF SCORES ON CRITERION 3 BY AGE GROUP AND SEX.

The List of Figures presents the headings exactly as they appear in the text.

# 21. Typing

Dissertations are presented in a typed form. Typefaces vary considerably and, if a typewriter is being used, the typeface must be not less than 2.0mm high with the x-height, which means the lower part of the letter, not less than 1.5mm. A 12 point typeface (12 characters to the inch) is the largest which can be used to ensure a workable number of words per line. Decorative typefaces should be avoided. The visual appearance is of some importance so, if using a typewriter, it is worth making sure that the machine to be used is in good condition and that the ribbon and carbons, if used, are new.

The same rules apply if the dissertation is being produced on a word-processor. The same font type and size should be used for all text throughout the dissertation. Examples of appropriate word-processor fonts include 12 point 'Times' and 'New Century Schoolbook'. Dissertations printed out on Dot Matrix printers are only acceptable if they are in 'Near Letter Quality' (NLQ). However, the regulations of the degree awarding body should be checked to ensure that Dot Matrix printed dissertations are acceptable.

Line spaces vary from typewriter to typewriter and, while it is normal for dissertations to be typed double-line spaced, with some machines one and a half-line spaces are acceptable. A further space should be allowed between paragraphs. The only occasions when single-line spacing is used are:

  (i) The Abstract
  (ii) Long, direct quotations
  (iii) Bibliographical entries
  (iv) Chapter, table, figure or appendix headings

Typewriters or word-processors with automatic spacing should be 'left justified'. Because of the limited number of words allowed by the dissertation margins, type that is right and left justified leaves awkward spaces and makes reading difficult.

Despite the cost, it is more than worthwhile to have a dissertation typed professionally. Employing a reliable and competent typist can save a great deal of anguish and frustration, particularly when working to a deadline. Before finalising an arrangement for typing, it is advisable to ask the typist to type a few pages to ensure that the accuracy and quality are acceptable.

At least three copies of a dissertation are normally required in addition to the first or 'top' copy. It is very rare nowadays for these copies to be carbon copies because not only are they an extra cost but also because they add to the time for typing and are subsequently difficult to correct or amend. Good quality photocopies, such as Xerox or Canon, are now accepted by most degree awarding bodies and have a number of advantages over carbon copies. In the first place, the first copy can be fully completed with any alterations made, the tables 'lined up', page numbers typed in and so on before the other copies are made. Secondly, photocopies can be made on paper of similar weight to that of the first copy and this makes the binding of the dissertation easier and cheaper. Thirdly, photocopies are of consistent quality whereas carbon copies tend to become increasingly blurred. It is also less time-consuming and cheaper to make photocopies of word processed dissertations than to produce the print-outs from the word processor.

Both the typist and the writer can be saved a lot of trouble by noting the following suggestions:

1.  The manuscript should be clearly written or, preferably, draft-typed. No matter how poorly typed in the first place, typescript is much easier for a typist to work from than manuscript.

2.  A typist works to instructions. Do not assume that he/she knows by some kind of intuition how the work is to be done. The layout and, particularly, anything unusual, should be

fully explained. Provide ruled-up pages as examples of margins, location of chapter headings and the placing of page numbers.

3. Be realistic about how long it will take for the typist to carry out the work. Space out the delivery of the manuscript to the typist, working backwards from the deadline date for the submission of the dissertation. The early chapters could be given to the typist as soon as they are in a final form. These could be being typed while, for instance, experimental work or analysis is still going on.

4. Keeping in close touch with the typist, particularly in the early stages, facilitates checking the typing quality, layout, spelling etc.

5. It is important to establish a professional working relationship with the typist. If the requirements have been made clear, work should not be accepted that does not meet these requirements.

An example of the basic requirements for typing is given on page 81.

When the dissertation is in its final typed form, it is the responsibility of the author to proofread the work. Proofreading can be tedious, particularly as the author has lived with material for a long time and often feels that he/she knows it word for word. However, proofreading is an important part of dissertation preparation and the author should try to detach himself/herself from the work, almost to the point of imagining that it has been written by someone else. If possible, get someone else to proofread the work as well. A fresh eye will often pick up points that would otherwise go unnoticed. The proofreading stage is not simply to check the accuracy of the typist regarding spelling and punctuation but it also provides a final opportunity to check for consistency, logic and the appropriateness of the organisation of ideas and data. The author needs to be quite ruthless, even at this late stage, in making revisions or amendments when they are necessary. It is worth remembering that the next reader is likely to be an examiner.

# 22. Binding

Dissertations are normally required to be bound prior to submission for examination. Some degree-awarding institutions, however, permit dissertations to be submitted in a 'semi-permanent' binding, which is a glued spine form within a soft cover, or in a loose-leaf form (provided they are securely held together such as in a spring-back binder) and not required to be bound in hard covers until after acceptance. This provision, of course, is particularly helpful should any amendments or alterations be required by the examiners.

Bindings should be of a fixed type so that pages cannot be removed or replaced. The front and back boards need to be of sufficient thickness to support the weight of the dissertation when it is standing upright. If the dissertation as a single volume would exceed 70mm thickness it should be bound as two or more volumes. Dissertations should be covered in cloth or linen which should be of a colour approved by the institution.

The title of the dissertation, the name and initials of the author, the qualification and the year of submission must appear on the *front* board of the dissertation. A normal requirement is that the title should be in 'at least 24pt. type' but, with approval, a smaller typeface may be used if the title is too long for this size to be visually acceptable. The name and initials of the author, the qualification and the year of submission must be tooled on the *spine*. If the dissertation comprises more than one volume, the volume number must also be placed on the spine. Lettering on the spine is normally horizontal when the dissertation is standing upright but may be placed along the spine if the dissertation is too thin to carry horizontal letters. In this case, the letters must be upright when the dissertation is lying on its back. Unless an institution has specific regulations, the layout for the lettering on a dissertation cover should be as shown in Figure 7. Lettering is normally tooled in gold.

Preferably, dissertations should be bound by a commercial bookbinder who is experienced in binding academic work. Supervisors should be asked to recommend suitable bookbinders. The bookbinder should be consulted at an early stage if it is intended to include unusual material such as folded pages or appendix material which needs to have a pocket made in the rear cover.

If the submission includes a substantial amount of bulky non-textual material, such as records of visual material or other practical work submitted for assessment, that cannot be accommodated in a pocket in the rear cover of the dissertation, it may be necessary to have a suitable case made. Whenever possible, the size of the front cover of the case should be the same as the dissertation but, if the material dictates it, it may be necessary for it to be larger. In all cases, the bookbinder should be asked to make a case that matches the dissertation binding, including the lettering. In these cases, the word 'Appendices' should be included on the spine and front cover.

| M.Phil | AN EMPIRICAL STUDY OF THE<br>PERSONALITY CHARACTERISTICS<br>OF SOME CHEMISTRY STUDENTS<br>IN COLLEGES OF FURTHER EDUCATION |
| J.BROWN | J. BROWN<br><br>MASTER OF PHILOSOPHY |
| 1980 | UNIVERSITY OF MIDCHESTER<br>1980 |

**Figure 7.** *Example of a binding layout*

# 23. Postscript

It will have become clear from the contents of this book that preparing a dissertation or thesis for submission for an academic award is a mixture of traditional practice, visual taste, common sense and meeting the requirements in regulations. To the inexperienced research reporter, all or any of these can be more than a little obscure and, if not obscure, at least pedantic. This book, therefore, has been designed to clarify and explain a range of necessary detail that has to be dealt with, one way or another, in preparing a dissertation or thesis.

It is inevitable that new or unforeseen problems in dissertation preparation will occur. The author would very much appreciate any information or queries on such problems from researchers who have used the book so that subsequent editions can provide as comprehensive a support as possible to initiates in this field.

# 24. Instructions for Typists

*These instructions may be copied and given to the typist.*

1. Paper size    A4

2. Margins
   | | |
   |---|---|
   | Top and right hand margin | 20mm |
   | Left hand margin | 40mm |
   | Bottom margin | 40mm |

   Exception – the first page of each chapter has a top margin of 40mm.

3. Page numbers    Page numbers are to be 20mm from the bottom edge of the page and central between the margins (110mm from the left hand edge of the page).

4. Type    Typographical style must be consistent throughout the whole dissertation.

   4.1 Normal lines of text are typed double-spaced with three line spaces between paragraphs.

   4.2 Single line spaces are used in:
      4.2.1 long quotations, which are also indented four characters from each margin.

      4.2.2 Chapter, table, figure and appendix headings when longer than one line.

      4.2.3 the Abstract.

      4.2.4 bibliographical entries, which are also inset four characters on the second and subsequent lines. Double-line spaces are used between entries in the Bibliography.

   4.3 Capital letters are used throughout for chapter, table, figure and appendix headings.

**Examples of bibliographical entries**

Arnheim, R. (1966). *Towards a Psychology of Art*. London: Faber and Faber.

Arnheim, R. (1970). *Visual Thinking*. London: Faber and Faber.

British Standards Institute (1990). *Recommendations for the presentation of theses and dissertations*. BS 4821. London: British Standards Institute.

Douglas, J. M. B., Ross, J. M., and Simpson, H. R. (1968). *All our Future*. London: Davies.

Erhard, W. (1985). *Effective action and accomplishment*. (Audio Cassette Recording). San Francisco, CA.: Audiotapes.

Fayerweather, J. (1960). Personal Relations. *In* Weinshall, T. D. (Ed.) (1977). *Culture and Management*. Harmondsworth: Penguin. 107–135.

Feldman, E. B. (1973). The Teacher as Model Critic. *J. Aesth. Educ.* 7, 1, 50–58.

Hannigan, J. A. (1980). Fragmentation in Science: The Case of Futurology. *Sociology. Rev.* 28, 2, 317–32.

Kaufman, I. (1971). The Art of Curriculum Making in the Arts. *In* Eisner, E. W. (Ed.). *Confronting Curriculum Reform*. Boston: Little Brown and Co. 91–112.

Li, X. and Crane, N. (1995). *Bibliographic Formats for Citing Electronic Information*. http://www.uvm.edu/~xli/reference/estyles.html. (15 July1996).

# Further Reading

Allison, B., O'Sullivan, T., Owen, A., Rice, J., Rothwell, A. and Saunders, C. (1996). *Research Skills for Students*. London: Kogan Page.

Allison, B. (Ed). (1996). *Allison Research Index of Research in Art and Design* (2nd edit.). (CD ROM). Leicester: ARIAD Associates.

American Psychological Association. (1994). *Publication Manual of the American Psychological Association* (4th edit.). Washington, DC: American Psychological Association.

Barnet, S. (1993). *A Short Guide to Writing about Art* (4th edit.). New York: Harper Collins.

Bellquist, J. E. (1993). *A Guide to Grammar and Usage for Psychology and Related Fields*. Hove: Lawrence Erlbaum Associates Ltd.

British Standards Institute (1990). *Recommendations for the Presentation of Theses and Dissertations*. BS 4821. London: British Standards Institute.

Chaplin, E. (1994). *Sociology and Visual Representation*. London: Routledge.

Day, R. A. (1989). *How to Write and Publish a Scientific Paper* (3rd edit.). Cambridge: Cambridge University Press.

*Dissertation Abstracts International*. (1969–). Ann Arbour, Michigan: University Microfilms International.

Fabb, N. and Durant, A. (1987). *How to Write Essays, Dissertations and Theses in Literary Studies*. Harlow: Longman.

Figuera, P. E. (1980). *Writing Research Reports*. Rediguide No. 23. Nottingham: University of Nottingham School of Education.

Fleisher, E. B. (1978). *A Style Manual for Citing Microform and Nonprint Media*. Chicago: American Library Association.

Furst, E J. (1990). *Writing Requirement for the Doctorate in Education*. Lanham, MD: University Press of America.

Gibaldi, J. (1995). *MLA Handbook: For Writers of Research Papers* (4th edit.). New York: Modern Language Association of America.

Hyams, M (Ed). (annual). *Aslib Index to Theses*. London: Aslib.

Li, X. and Crane, N. (1996). *Electronic Style: A Guide to Citing Electronic Information*. (Rev. edit.). Westport, CT: Mecklermedia.

Patrias, K. (1991). *National Library of Medicine Recommended Formats for Bibliographic Citation*. Bethesda, MD: National Library of Medicine.

Phillips, E. M. and Pugh, D. S. (1995). *How to Get a Ph.D.* (2nd edit.). Milton Keynes: Open University Press.

Van Dalen, D. B. (1966). *Understanding Educational Research*. New York: McGraw Hill.

Van Leunen, M-C. (1978). *A Handbook for Scholars*. New York: Knopf.

Watson, G. (1987). *Writing a Thesis: A Guide to Long Essays and Dissertations*. Harlow: Longman.

# Index

## Also available from Kogan Page

*Creating Your Career*, Simon Kent

*Great Answers to Tough Interview Questions: How to Get the Job You Want (3rd edition)*, Martin John Yate

*How to Pass Graduate Recruitment Tests*, Mike Bryon

*How to Pass Numeracy Tests*, Harry Tolley and Ken Thomas

*How to Pass Selection Tests*, Mike Bryon and Sanjay Modha

*How to Pass Technical Selection Tests*, Mike Bryon and Sanjay Modha

*How to Pass the Civil Service Qualifying Tests*, Mike Bryon

*How to Pass Verbal Reasoning Tests*, Harry Tolley and Ken Thomas

*How You Can Get That Job! Application Forms and Letters Made Easy*, Rebecca Corfield

*How to Win as a Part-Time Student*, Tom Bourner and Phil Race

*Job Hunting Made Easy (3rd edition)*, John Bramham and David Cox

*Job Hunting after University or College*, Jan Perrett

*Preparing Your Own CV*, Rebecca Corfield

*Readymade Job Search Letters*, Lynn Williams

*Test Your Own Aptitude* (2nd edition), Jim Barrett and Geoff Williams

*Your First Job: Choosing, Getting and Keeping it*, Vivien Donald and Ray Grose